To:

Emily

Thank you for all
of your support!
Enjoy the book!

— Beth

"Outside of a dog, a book is man's best friend.
Inside of a dog, it's too dark to read."
- Groucho Marx

This book is dedicated to dog rescuers everywhere, especially those that work tirelessly to find pit bulls their forever homes. As we all know, the odds are stacked against them from the start. "Rescue" is more than just adoption, as there are dozens of ways to help rescue a homeless pet: fostering, donating, volunteering, … and the list goes on and on. Rescue dogs are not broken. They are worth it. Let's rescue on, one by one, until there are none.

First Printing, 2016

ISBN-13: 978-0692696002

ISBN-10: 0692696008

Bully Pulpit Press

Pennsylvania, USA

Email: BullyPulpitPress@yahoo.com

Liberty and Justice
Give Pits a Chance

Liberty and Justice are mastiff sisters. Like many sisters and brothers, they are very different, but each is special in her own ways. Liberty is the older sister. She's bigger and slower and, well,... drool-ier. She is such a lover and gives the biggest, sloppiest kisses with the most enormous tongue you've ever seen. She watches over everyone and everything, especially her little sister. She doesn't miss a trick.

Justice is skinnier and taller and full of energy. She runs around like she's got ants in her pants all the time. She's the baby in the family and she loves it that way. She knows she's cute and she uses her sweet baby face to melt everyone's heart. Both girls are adored by their family and have a happy life. They have it made in the shade.

But one night, the girls' parents were heard talking about adopting another dog. He was old and sick and wasn't doing well in the shelter. They said he was a "pit bull" and he needed to get out of that dirty, cold shelter right away if he were ever going to feel better.

Justice dropped the bone she was chewing and sat straight up. She didn't like what she was hearing. SHE is the baby in the house! They can't get a new brother! Will her parents still love her as much as they do now? What if they didn't have time for her anymore? Will she have to share her toys with TWO siblings? Justice was getting nervous!

Liberty was also a little uneasy. She wasn't afraid of getting a new sibling though. She knew that her parents still love her the same, even after Justice came along. She liked having a sister and she wouldn't mind having another brother or sister. But she WAS scared about her parents adopting a PIT BULL. Liberty had heard all kinds of scary things about pit bulls. She had heard that pit bulls were mean and that they like to fight other dogs. Liberty didn't want to fight. And she didn't want a mean dog in their home. Oh no! This was such bad news!

Though the girls had heard of pit bulls, they had never met one. They have had fun with many types of dogs, including their friend Maggie, the Bulldog. She is a lot like Liberty, with lots of wrinkles and a slow pace. Their cousin dog, Mia, is a hunting dog. She taught the girls how to chase birds like a pro.

Harley is a handsome, black, furry mixed breed rescue dog who lives with the girls' Gram and Pap. He likes to run around with Justice until their tongues droop almost to the ground. Their friend Jasper, the Vizsla, likes to swim. The girls could swim and splash in the water for hours with Jasper. They have all of these wonderful dog friends, but not one of them is a pit bull. They are nervous to meet a pit bull, let alone live with one!

A few days later, the girls'
parents brought home a soft,
new dog bed, a couple of new
dog toys, and a new collar. Uh
oh! It looked like the new pit
bull was coming home, and
coming home soon! Justice
started hiding all of her toys so
she wouldn't have to share
them with the new dog.
Liberty practiced looking scary,
showing her teeth and fluffing
up the hair on her back, in case
she had to protect her parents
and sister from a mean pit bull.
This was going to be hard for
her. Liberty had never been
mean before and she wasn't
sure if she could do it.

The next day, their parents brought home the new dog! He was a 12-year-old pit bull and was nothing but skin and bones. He was kind of smelly and dirty. He had a cold and was coughing and sneezing all the time. One ear stood up and the other one flopped down. What a mess this dog was! Why would the girls' parents bring home a smelly old dog from the shelter when they could buy a fluffy, cute puppy at the pet store? The girls just couldn't understand it.

For the next several days, the parents kept the new dog separate from the girls so they wouldn't catch his cold. The parents bathed the new dog, brushed his hair, cut his toenails, and cleaned his ears. The girls watched as their parents took good care of this new dog, whom they called "Perry". They fed him healthy food and took him to the vet for a check up and some medicine for his cold. Justice was happy that despite all the care the new dog was getting, her parents still spent time with her. From the other side of the gate, Liberty was watching Perry like a hawk! She wanted to make sure he was not being mean to her parents. To her surprise, he was very loving and gentle with them.

Before long, the skinny, stinky pit bull had gained a few pounds, had a beautiful, clean coat, and had gotten over his cold. It was time to allow him to meet his new sisters, nose to nose. Justice held onto her favorite toy tightly, concerned that her new brother would take it. Liberty was so nervous! She knew she had to keep her family safe, but she didn't want to fight with her new brother. Perry was allowed out into the yard with the rest of the family. The three dogs all sniffed each other from one end to the other. Liberty was relieved that Perry didn't want to fight. Justice allowed him to smell her favorite toy, but he didn't try to take it.

Their dad threw a ball to Perry and he fetched it like a good dog would. He then threw the ball to Justice and then to Liberty. Each dog had their turn playing with their parents. They played tug, wrestled in the grass, and chased each other around the yard. They shared the toys and each got plenty of attention from the people they love.

Like any dog, Perry needed some training and his parents had to teach him right from wrong. They trained him without yelling or spanking him, but rather rewarded him with treats when he was behaving well. They knew it was important to be patient with Perry as he was learning the rules of his new house. He was a quick learner and he loved to make his new parents proud of him.

Liberty and Justice knew that two dogs could have fun together, but they were realizing that three dogs could have a blast (and find even more mischief)! The girls were too big to squeeze under the bushes to chase out the bunny that lived under there... but Perry wasn't. After Perry chased out the bunny, all three dogs would run after her. She was much faster than the dogs and would always easily escape. The dogs didn't want to hurt her, but they enjoyed the chase.

Liberty and Justice loved to eat apples from the tree in the yard. But they could only eat the apples that fell off the tree. They were often mushy and had bugs in them. YUCK! Now with Perry's help, they could swipe fresh apples straight from the tree. Since Perry was older and wiser, he reminded the girls to spit out the apple seeds because they can make dogs sick. The girls never knew that, which might explain all the belly aches they got when they ate the apples before. Liberty and Justice were realizing that there are benefits to having a smart older brother!

Perry had several rescued pit bull friends that he met at the shelter. They soon became friends of the girls as well. Tyson is brindle-colored like Justice. She thinks that he is cute and has a bit of a crush on him. Jasmine is black and brindle too. She lives with another dog and even a cat! Misty is gray with super tall ears that make her look a lot like a rabbit. Koopa is brown and white. He has a human sister that is a lot of fun and he also has a human baby in his family. He loves both of those girls very much.

All of these new pit bull friends are fun to play with. They aren't mean. They are able to live peacefully with kids, other dogs, and even cats! The girls could not imagine living with a cat and not chasing it! While pit bulls may not be a perfect fit for every home, it's clear that they can be wonderful family pets in many situations, if given a chance. They just need responsible parents who know about the needs of these special dogs.

Liberty felt bad that she once thought pit bulls were bad dogs. She now had many good friends that were pit bulls. She should not have judged Perry before she even met him. Justice was sorry that she didn't want to share her toys or her parents' attention with her new brother. She was still loved by her parents the same as before. They still played with her and cared for her. She still had toys of her own and some that she shared. Getting a new sibling wasn't really that bad. In fact, she kind of liked having one sister AND one brother!

Liberty and Justice had grown very fond of their new brother. Although Perry was much older than the girls, he still was quite spunky and full of life. And even though he came from a shelter, smelly and sick, with some proper care, he became healthy and handsome. Liberty and Justice were thankful that their parents chose to adopt Perry. They knew that many people would have passed him up because he was older and not a puppy. And a lot of people may not have wanted him simply because he is a pit bull or because he was sick and shabby-looking. Their parents, and now the girls, realized that he deserves a good home as much as any other dog or puppy from a store or breeder.

There are so many nice dogs in shelters waiting for good homes, but sadly they are often over-looked. Perry was not overlooked though. He was adopted and is loved. He will never go back to a cold and scary shelter. He has tried to be a good example for pit bulls everywhere. He tries to meet many people, young and old, and show them that he is a good boy. He wants them to see that they don't have to fear pit bulls just because of their breed. He hopes to convince people that pit bulls deserve a chance at a good life too. It is important that they are properly trained and treated kindly, but a pit bull is a dog, not a monster!

Like any older brother, Perry has continued to teach his sisters new things...

like how to get hugs by jumping into the mail truck with Jackie, the mail lady...

...and how to completely destroy a stuffed toy in under 2 minutes!

The End

Stop, "*Paws*" and Rewind!

Can you find the paw prints hidden in the story?

There is one paw print on each page.

Signed, With Love!

Perry

Liberty

Justice

The Real Liberty, Justice, & Perry

WHEN PERRY WAS
FIRST ADOPTED

Pit Bull Facts: (for kids AND adults)

- A "pit bull" is a type of dog that includes several breeds with similar physical traits. Some 40% of all shelter dogs are labeled as "Bully Breeds."

- Pit bulls are notoriously fond of children. They are sturdy, energetic, tolerant, and extremely patient. As with any dog, children should be supervised and be taught proper ways to interact with dogs. Children should never, NEVER sit on, stand on, or tease ANY DOG, especially while it is sleeping or eating.

- American Pit Bull Terriers score better (86.8%) on American Temperament Test Society evaluations than Beagles (80%), Golden Retrievers (85.2%), and many other common "family" dogs. They consistently fall into the category of one of the top 5 most stable dogs.

- Sergeant Stubby was a pit bull that saved the lives of American men in World War I. He was trained to salute his Army officers and was said to have captured a German spy by the seat of his pants!

Educate.

Don't Discriminate!

Funny Bone

- Why are Dalmatians no good at playing Hide and Seek?

    ~ Because they are always spotted

- Why did the dog fall into the well?

    ~He couldn't see that well

- What do you do if you lose your dog in the forest?

    ~ Put your ear up to a tree and listen for the bark

- What did the cowboy say when his dog ran away?

    ~ "Well, doggone!"

- What do you do when your dog chews up the dictionary?

    ~ Take the words out of her mouth

Don't forget to check out *Liberty and Justice for Paul*, the first book in this series!

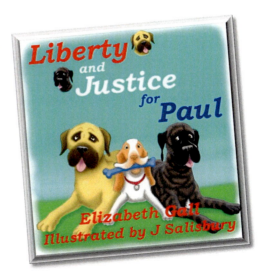

Run Free with the Angels, Perry Boy

19 Dec 2000 - 18 May 2016

Two weeks prior to publishing, Perry crossed the Rainbow Bridge at the age of 15 years.

He will live forever in our hearts as the handsome, loving, and cherished boy that we adored.

Made in the USA
Middletown, DE
28 May 2016